Bewitching Britain

The Hidden Witches of England

By Lee Brickley

Copyright 2023 @LeeBrickley

Contents:

Introduction 5

Unveiling Pendle: Lancashire's Twelve 11

Alice Nutter: A Lady Among Witches 17

Jane Wenham: The Witch of Walkern 23

The Bideford Witches: The End of an Era 29

Elizabeth Southerns: The Matron of Pendle 35

Anne, Joan, and Ellen: The Leicester Witches 41

The Witchfinder General: Matthew Hopkins 47

The Berwick Witches: Mass Hysteria 53

Mother Shipton: The Prophetess of Knaresborough 57

Agnes Waterhouse: The First Witch of Chelmsford 63

The St Osyth Witches: The Accursed Town 69

Elizabeth Sawyer: The Witch of Edmonton 73

The Witches of Warboys 79

Cunning Folk and Pellers: The Other Side of the Coin 85

Elizabeth Clarke: Hopkins' First Victim 91

Daemonologie: Witchcraft from a Royal Perspective............97

The Case of Eleanor Cobham: Witchcraft in the Court........103

The Witches of Belvoir: A Noble Family's Curse...................109

Margaret Jourdemayne: Witch of Eye Next Westminster.115

The Mompesson Haunting: Witchcraft or Ghost Story?....121

Witches of the New Forest: The Burley Coven.......................127

Afterword..133

About The Author..139

Introduction

Every land has its lore, every culture its myths and legends, every corner of this world its tales of the extraordinary. Some of these narratives permeate the landscape, resonating through centuries, whispering in the wind, and flowing with the river streams. The British Isles, and England in particular, are such places where the veil between the realms of the seen and unseen, the ordinary and the extraordinary, the human and the mystical, often thins. A prime example of these extraordinary narratives is the tales of English witches.

The term 'witch' itself has metamorphosed throughout history, oscillating between reverence and fear, respect and repugnance. In ancient times, witches were considered wise women, healers, and seers, their intimate knowledge of herbs, nature, and celestial bodies making them indispensable in their communities. However, with the advent of Christianity, their image began to darken. Witches became synonymous with the devil and evil. These transformations were dictated by the societal, religious, and political contexts of different epochs, and thus the notion of the witch became an enigma, a point of contention, and a symbol of the struggle between old and new, nature and civilization, female autonomy and patriarchal control.

'Bewitching Britain: The Hidden Witches of England' is a journey through time and space, through forests and over moors, across centuries and socio-religious paradigms, following the intricate and compelling narrative of English witchcraft. The book seeks to delve beyond the traditional, often sensationalised accounts of witches as malevolent hags or beautiful enchantresses, to uncover the truth of their existence, their stories, and their impact on English culture and society.

Each chapter of this book explores a different account of English witchcraft, unearthing the hidden tales of real men and women who, for one reason or another, were embroiled in the complex web of witchcraft. These individuals range from the infamous witches of Pendle Forest, who were caught up in the hysteria of the 1612 witch trials, to Cunning Murrell, the 19th-century cunning man whose folk magic and wisdom made him a respected figure in his community. We will traverse the fascinating world of Mother Shipton, the prophetic witch, venture into the chilling practices of Isobel Gowdie, and dare to face the cunning witchery of the wise woman from Burley in the New Forest.

The book will also explore the places known for their witchy associations: the eerily tranquil Lancaster where the Pendle witches lived and died, the charming village of Warboys, home to the notorious Throckmorton witches, and the stunning beauty of the New Forest, which still resonates with the energy of ancient magic. As we travel through these places and stories, we will not only encounter witch trials, cunning folk, and wise women, but we will also unravel the profound meaning that these witches held for their contemporaries and the lasting legacy they have left in their wake.

Yet, these tales are not merely historical accounts of individual witches. They are, in essence, the tales of a society grappling with change and the unknown. They are narratives of fear and misunderstanding, of persecution and survival, and ultimately, of transformation and acceptance.

While we navigate these stories, it's important to note that the concept of 'witch' is layered and complex, reflecting not only the individual witch's intentions but also the societal and religious anxieties and expectations of the time. We will see that the figure of the witch has evolved dramatically over the centuries - from the feared and persecuted in the Middle Ages and Early Modern Period, through a period of disbelief and ridicule, to a newfound acceptance and revival in modern times.

Through 'Bewitching Britain: The Hidden Witches of England', you are invited to view the landscape of England through a different lens, to see beneath the surface of charming villages, ancient forests, and foggy moors, to uncover the tales of extraordinary individuals who dared to live their truth in a world that refused to understand them.

It is my hope that as we journey through the hidden paths of England's witchy past, we may find a deeper understanding of what it truly means to be a witch, a deeper compassion for those who suffered, and a deeper appreciation for the intricate tapestry that is the history of English witchcraft.

So, as we prepare to embark on this journey, I invite you to suspend your disbelief, open your mind to the extraordinary, and step into the magical landscape of witchy England. Welcome to 'Bewitching Britain: The Hidden Witches of England'. Let the journey begin.

Unveiling Pendle: Lancashire's Twelve

In the verdant, rolling landscape of Lancashire, a striking silhouette emerges from the hills. The Hill of Pendle, its peak often shrouded in a ghostly mist, stands as a brooding testament to the region's rich and tumultuous past. It is here, beneath the sombre shadow of Pendle Hill, that one of the most infamous episodes of English witchcraft unfurled: the Pendle witch trials.

As we embark on our journey through the annals of England's witchy past, there is no better place to start than Pendle. The events that transpired here in the early 17th century encapsulate the palpable fear, prejudice, and superstition that punctuated this era of witch hysteria.

The Pendle witch trials began under the reign of King James I, a monarch known for his obsession with the supernatural and particularly the dark arts. King James himself penned 'Daemonologie,' a book expounding his belief in witchcraft and demonology, that laid the groundwork for the witch-hunts that would sweep across England.

The year was 1612, a time when the fear of witches and their malevolent magic hung heavy in the air. In Pendle, a place already steeped in folkloric superstitions, the whispers of witchcraft were soon to reach a fever pitch. The events leading to the trial started innocently enough, with an encounter between a local peddler, John Law, and a destitute woman, Alizon Device. Alizon, upon being refused help by the peddler, cursed him out of frustration and desperation. Not long after, Law suffered a stroke.

Coincidence, one might think, but in the superstitious minds of the 17th-century Lancashire locals, it was perceived as a sinister act of witchcraft. Alizon was apprehended, and under the duress of interrogation, she confessed to the crime of witchcraft and implicated others, including members of her own family. The list of the accused soon grew, spiralling into a maelström of paranoia, accusation, and recrimination. Thus, the stage was set for one of the most notorious witch trials in British history.

Alizon Device belonged to a family living on the margins of society, feared and shunned by their neighbours. Her mother, Elizabeth Device, and her grandmother, known as Old Demdike, were long reputed to be witches. Now, joined by their neighbours, Anne Whittle (also known as Old Chattox) and her daughter Anne Redferne, and several others, they found themselves at the centre of a dangerous whirlwind. In total, twelve were accused - the Lancashire Twelve.

In their testimonies, these individuals confessed to an astonishing array of crimes. They spoke of maleficium - causing harm through witchcraft, of making clay figures to harm their enemies, of nocturnal meetings where they feasted with familiar spirits and of desecrating holy sacraments. The vivid and lurid details that emerged during the trials painted a terrifying tableau of witchcraft that sent shockwaves through the community and beyond.

Among the accused, perhaps the most chilling account was that of Old Demdike. Regarded as the matriarch of the Pendle witches, she was described as a woman who had trafficked with a familiar spirit for decades. This spirit, Tibb, would often appear in the guise of a little boy and do her bidding in exchange for her soul. Old Demdike's reported admission of her pact with Tibb marked a critical turning point in the trial, as it embodied the Church and the State's worst fears about witches – that they renounced Christianity and held allegiance with the Devil himself.

Presiding over this extraordinary trial was Judge Altham and Sir Edward Bromley, men who were driven by duty, fear, and an unwavering belief in the reality of witchcraft. Using King James's Daemonologie as their guide, they navigated the testimonies and confessions of the accused, their judgement clouded by prevailing superstitions.

The trial lasted for two days, at the end of which ten of the Lancashire Twelve were found guilty. The condemned included Elizabeth Device, Anne Whittle, Anne Redferne, and several others. They were hanged at Gallows Hill in Lancaster in August 1612. Old Demdike, the elderly matriarch of the group, died in prison awaiting trial.

The Pendle witch trials remain etched in history, not just for the tragic deaths they led to, but also for the light they shed on the society and psyche of 17th-century England. These events were emblematic of a time of societal upheaval, fear of the unknown, and the shifting tides of religious beliefs.

Today, the shadowy spectre of Pendle's past continues to loom over its beautiful landscape. The hill, the villages, and the very air seem to whisper the stories of the Lancashire Twelve. The tale of these individuals and the witch trials serve as a stark reminder of a time when fear and misunderstanding guided justice, casting a dark shadow over the annals of English history.

Through the lens of the Pendle witch trials, we glimpse the complex tapestry of English witchcraft, rife with fear, prejudice, and superstition. It sets the stage for our exploration into the rich, complex, and often unsettling history of witches in England. As we peel back the layers of the past, we will discover that the narrative of witchcraft is as diverse and intricate as the men and women who lived and died under its name.

Alice Nutter: A Lady Among Witches

Alice Nutter is a name that resonates among the corridors of English witchcraft history. Her involvement in the Pendle witch trials marks an enigmatic episode, filled with mystery, intrigue, and profound sociopolitical implications. As we immerse ourselves further in our exploration of English witchcraft, Alice Nutter's case presents an intriguing deviation from the societal norms of the 17th century. A woman of substantial wealth and social standing, Alice's story defies the typical profile of those usually accused of witchcraft.

In the annals of witch-hunting across Europe and England, the accused were often individuals on the margins of society - the poor, the old, the infirm, and those bearing the brunt of societal prejudice. However, Alice Nutter, a lady of genteel birth, broke this mould, which serves to deepen the mystery surrounding her involvement in the Pendle witch trials.

To comprehend Alice's unusual circumstances, we need to look at her life prior to the trials. Alice hailed from a well-respected, land-owning family in Roughlee, Pendle. The Nutters were prosperous, owning vast tracts of farmland and, unlike the other accused, Alice did not bear the brunt of abject poverty. She lived in a comfortable stone house, a far cry from the hovels of her co-accused. Yet, amidst the throes of witch-hysteria that gripped Lancashire, Alice found herself swept up in a tide of suspicion and paranoia.

The first question that arises is why Alice, a woman of status, would find herself accused of witchcraft. Some have suggested that her indictment was not a result of actual involvement in witchcraft but rather a byproduct of long-standing feuds among the gentry families of Lancashire. The period was rife with social and religious upheaval, the echoes of the Reformation still fresh, and the tensions between Catholic and Protestant factions ran high. Some theorise that Alice, whose family was rumoured to be secret Catholics, might have been a victim of these religious skirmishes.

However, another thread in the tapestry of Alice Nutter's story is her presence at Malkin Tower on Good Friday, 1612. Malkin Tower, home to the Device family, was the purported venue of a witches' meeting, a gathering which played a central role in the trials. Alice's presence there was corroborated by several testimonies, including those of the Device family themselves. This event, infamously referred to as the 'Good Friday Gathering', was critical in consolidating the case against the Pendle witches.

It is worth noting that Alice's behaviour during the trials further set her apart from her co-accused. She maintained a resolute silence, neither confessing to witchcraft nor implicating others. This was a stark contrast to the other accused, whose confessions and testimonies, often obtained under duress, wove a convoluted web of accusations. Alice's silence can be interpreted in several ways. It may have been a desperate act of self-preservation, a defiant stance against false accusations, or a quiet assertion of her innocence.

In the end, despite her status, Alice Nutter was found guilty of witchcraft. She was executed at Gallows Hill in Lancaster alongside the other condemned witches from the trial. The mystery surrounding her involvement and her stoic silence until the end adds an air of intrigue and tragic dignity to her story.

Alice Nutter's tale is a vivid reminder that the witch-hunts were not solely a war against the marginalised or the weak; they were a societal phenomenon, influenced by a complex interplay of politics, religion, and social dynamics. In many ways, Alice's story encapsulates the paranoia and fear that permeated English society during this period.

Even centuries later, the tale of Alice Nutter continues to captivate and intrigue. She is commemorated in her home village of Roughlee, where a statue stands in her memory, a poignant tribute to her life and the tumultuous period she lived in.

As we turn the pages of England's witchcraft history, we encounter stories that are as varied as they are chilling. Alice Nutter, a lady among witches, presents a tale that defies conventions, offering a glimpse into the social and political dimensions of the witch hunts. Her story serves as a stark reminder that fear, when fuelled by misunderstanding and prejudice, can breach all boundaries of class and privilege. It compels us to look beyond the surface, to question, and to seek the nuanced truths hidden beneath the broad strokes of history. Alice's story may be but a single thread in the intricate tapestry of English witchcraft, yet it adds a depth and complexity that can't be overlooked in our exploration of this fascinating subject.

Jane Wenham: The Witch of Walkern

Jane Wenham: a name etched in the annals of English witchcraft history as one of the last people to be convicted of witchcraft. The case, which unfolded in the small village of Walkern, Hertfordshire, in the early 18th century, is notable for the controversy it ignited, setting clerics, intellectuals, and law enforcement officials at odds. Jane Wenham's story paints a fascinating portrait of the changing perceptions of witchcraft in England during this time.

Born around 1644, Jane lived most of her life in Walkern, a place no different from hundreds of other quiet, unassuming English villages. However, beneath the tranquillity, the threads of superstition, envy, and mistrust wove a complicated social tapestry. Jane, a widow, lived alone and, like many isolated, elderly women of the time, was a prime target for accusations of witchcraft.

The spark that would ignite Jane's trial was seemingly innocuous. A quarrel over some straw with her landlord, Matthew Gilston, quickly escalated into a full-blown witchcraft allegation when Jane was accused of bewitching workers, causing them to suffer fits and other unusual ailments. It's worth noting that Matthew Gilston had a history of levelling witchcraft accusations. The social dynamics of small communities like Walkern often allowed personal grievances to grow into sinister allegations.

The accusations against Jane Wenham culminated in a trial in 1712, presided over by Sir John Powell. Despite the lack of concrete evidence and the shaky testimonies of alleged victims, Jane was found guilty. Sir John Powell, although clearly uncomfortable with the proceedings, had little choice but to pass the sentence dictated by the Witchcraft Act of 1604 – death by hanging.

However, Jane's story doesn't end here. Sir John Powell, who had openly expressed scepticism during the trial, granted her a reprieve. He used his influence to petition Queen Anne, who ultimately granted Jane a royal pardon, sparing her from the gallows. This act set a groundbreaking precedent and highlighted the growing doubts about the legitimacy of witch trials among the educated elites.

What makes Jane Wenham's case particularly significant is the ensuing public discourse. Her trial triggered a fervent debate, not just in Hertfordshire, but across the whole of England. Pamphlets and treatises discussing her case were published and widely circulated, essentially turning Jane's ordeal into a nationwide talking point.

The case of Jane Wenham marked a point of divergence, a period of transition in English society's views on witchcraft. The scepticism and discomfort expressed by Judge Powell echoed the sentiments of a growing segment of society that had started questioning the reality of witchcraft and the legitimacy of such trials. These individuals, many of whom were figures of authority and influence, played pivotal roles in steering the discourse on witchcraft towards a more rational, enlightened direction.

However, the public debate ignited by Jane's trial also exposed the tenacious grip of superstition on English society. Even as intellectuals and clergymen voiced their doubts, many, particularly among the rural population, held steadfastly onto their beliefs in witches and their malevolent powers. The duality of this response reflects the broader social and intellectual transition of the period.

Jane Wenham, after her reprieve, lived a relatively quiet life. However, she remained a figure of fear and suspicion within her community. Shunned by her neighbours, she found refuge in the house of the sympathetic local rector, Reverend Francis Bragge, where she lived until her death in 1730.

As we trace the path of witchcraft history in England, the story of Jane Wenham offers valuable insights. It highlights the profound societal transformations of the period, the struggle between traditional beliefs and emerging enlightenment ideals. It brings to light the changing perceptions of witchcraft, the growing scepticism, and the persistent superstition that encapsulates the complex and often paradoxical nature of this chapter in English history.

Moreover, the story of Jane Wenham serves as a reminder of the human cost of witchcraft hysteria. A widow, living in isolation, became a target for fear, suspicion, and social scapegoating. The Witch of Walkern's tale is not just a study of societal change; it is a human story, marked by fear, prejudice, and ultimately, a struggle for survival. It is stories like these that emphasise the importance of looking beyond the grand narratives, delving deeper into individual lives that illuminate the broader historical landscape.

From the wealthy Alice Nutter to the humble Jane Wenham, we find that witchcraft accusations transcended social status. Each story contributes to a more holistic understanding of the phenomena of witch hunts, highlighting the complex interplay of social, political, and personal factors that fuelled the witchcraft hysteria.

The tale of Jane Wenham, the Witch of Walkern, serves as a stark reminder of a darker time in England's past. As we explore further into the annals of English witchcraft history, each account offers a unique perspective, further enriching our understanding of this intriguing and complex subject.

The Bideford Witches: The End of an Era

In the annals of English witchcraft, the story of the Bideford witches occupies a significant place. Temperance Lloyd, Mary Trembles, and Susannah Edwards, three elderly women from the port town of Bideford in Devon, hold the melancholic distinction of being the last witches to be executed in England. Their story marks the end of an era, a grim reminder of a time when fear and superstition could lead to deadly outcomes.

Temperance Lloyd, the first of the three to be accused, was an elderly widow known for her peculiar behaviour, which made her a subject of suspicion in the local community. The initial accusations against Temperance came from her neighbour, Grace Thomas, who claimed to be suffering from a mysterious illness. Grace reported that she had seen Temperance's spirit leaving her body and had been tormented by the spectre ever since. Grace Thomas's claims, backed by her husband's testimony, marked the beginning of Temperance's ordeal.

When Temperance was interrogated, she confessed to the crimes of conversing with the devil and causing harm to Grace Thomas through witchcraft. The confession, undoubtedly extracted under duress, was made in the presence of the Mayor and Justices of the Peace. Temperance's fate was sealed with her own words, as she implicated herself in the acts of witchcraft.

Soon after Temperance's confession, two other women from the community, Mary Trembles and Susannah Edwards, were also implicated. Mary was singled out after she was seen collecting water from a well known to be frequented by Temperance. Under interrogation, Mary confessed to witchcraft and implicated Susannah Edwards as the one who introduced her to the devil.

In August of 1682, all three women were put on trial at the Exeter Assizes, accused of causing harm through witchcraft. They were found guilty based on their confessions and the testimonies of their neighbours. The jury, made up of local gentry, showed no hesitation in convicting the three, and they were sentenced to death by hanging. A few days later, in front of a large crowd gathered on Heavitree gallows in Exeter, Temperance Lloyd, Mary Trembles, and Susannah Edwards were executed, marking the end of witch hangings in England.

However, the story of the Bideford witches doesn't just stop with their execution. It also throws light on the socio-cultural dynamics of the period. The fear of witchcraft persisted through the 17th century, despite a growing scepticism among the educated elites. The case of the Bideford witches underscores the pervasive power of fear and suspicion in a society caught between the vestiges of mediaeval superstition and the dawn of the Age of Enlightenment.

The fact that all three women were elderly and socially

vulnerable is telling. Throughout the history of witch persecutions, it was often those on the margins of society - the elderly, the poor, the widowed, and the solitary - who bore the brunt of accusations. The Bideford witches were no exception. Their social standing, or lack thereof, made them easy targets for the accusations of their more prosperous neighbours.

The trials and subsequent execution of the Bideford witches also serve to highlight the role of the law and local authorities in perpetuating the witch hysteria. In the case of Bideford, it was the local magistrates and gentry who played a decisive role in upholding the guilty verdict. The confessions extracted from the women under duress were accepted without question, and their fates were sealed based on spectral evidence, a type of evidence even then considered dubious and controversial.

The Bideford witch trials, while marking the end of an era, also marked the beginning of a change in society's attitude towards witchcraft. Following the executions, there was a noticeable shift in public sentiment, and subsequent witch trials often ended in acquittals, signalling a decline in the belief in witchcraft.

The tale of the Bideford witches is a vital piece of English history, a dark yet important chapter that holds lessons of tolerance, justice, and reason. While Temperance Lloyd, Mary Trembles, and Susannah Edwards may have been the last victims of witch hysteria in England, their story serves as a stark reminder of the power of fear and superstition and the importance of rationality and justice.

As we continue to explore the depth and breadth of witchcraft history in England, the story of the Bideford witches, laden with tragedy and caution, offers an understanding of how societal, cultural, and legal factors intersected in the history of witch trials. Their tale is a testament to the shifting perceptions of witchcraft in England, a narrative of a society in transition. As we delve deeper, each story further illuminates the complex tapestry of England's witchcraft history, laying bare the human stories beneath the overarching narrative of progress and change.

Elizabeth Southerns: The Matron of Pendle

Elizabeth Southerns, more commonly known by her nickname, "Old Demdike," is a figure of significant historical intrigue, a central character in the infamous Pendle witch trials of 1612. A woman aged over eighty, she had a reputation that preceded her, a reputation steeped in local lore and superstition. The head of the Demdike clan, Elizabeth was known and feared throughout Pendle as a witch, a healer, a cunning woman, and by some, a scapegoat.

Born around 1530, in a time when England was undergoing significant religious transformations, Elizabeth lived through the shift from Catholicism to Protestantism, a change that played a pivotal role in shaping her life and fate. In a region like Lancashire, where the old religion had a strong grip, Elizabeth, like many others, practised a blend of Catholicism and folk magic. These practices, tolerated for a while, would ultimately lead to her downfall as societal views began to shift.

Living in a decrepit old tower known as Malkin Tower with her daughter, grandson, and a friend, Elizabeth was seen as the matron of a community that existed on the fringes of society. Her clan, along with the Chattox family, were known practitioners of folk magic. To some, they were healers and wise women; to others, witches who could bring misfortune.

One of the defining aspects of Elizabeth Southerns was her knack for storytelling. She claimed to have a familiar, a spirit named Tibb, who appeared to her in different forms. According to her confessions, Tibb promised to help her in times of need, providing her with powers to heal and cause harm. These stories, passed down in hushed whispers, only added to her mystique.

But, when her granddaughter, Alizon Device, had a fateful

encounter with a peddler named John Law, the quiet lives of the Demdike and Chattox families changed forever. Alizon, following an argument with Law, cursed him, and when Law suffered a stroke shortly after, Alizon's guilt led her to confess to witchcraft, implicating her family and the Chattoxes in the process.

Arrested and brought before Roger Nowell, a local magistrate with a reputation for witch-hunting, Elizabeth, along with her family, was accused of causing harm through witchcraft. Elizabeth's age, her reputation as a healer, and her own confessions, worked against her. She confessed to having a familiar and causing harm, claims she may have initially made to enhance her standing as a cunning woman, but which now played a significant role in sealing her fate.

However, Elizabeth Southerns would never make it to trial. The harsh conditions of her imprisonment at Lancaster Castle, coupled with her advanced age, took their toll. She passed away in the gaol in 1612, before she could be brought to trial, yet her spectre loomed large over the proceedings. Her death did not lead to mercy for her family.

Her daughter, Elizabeth Device, and grandchildren, Alizon and James, were found guilty of witchcraft and executed.

Elizabeth Southerns's life and influence have remained subjects of interest for historians. She was a woman who lived on her terms, a matriarch who used her reputation to carve out a place for her family in a society that did not have much to offer them. Yet, it was this very reputation, the rumours, and the stories, that ultimately led to her family's downfall.

To understand the life of Elizabeth Southerns is to understand the era she lived in. Her story is a window into a time and place where folk magic and Catholicism intertwined, where societal and religious changes painted cunning folk as witches, and where fear of the unknown led to tragic outcomes. As we explore more about the witches of England, the story of Elizabeth Southerns offers valuable insights into the lives of those accused and the social conditions that allowed such witch-hunts to thrive.

From the decrepit Malkin Tower to the cold, unforgiving

cells of Lancaster Castle, Elizabeth Southerns's journey is one of resilience, fear, power, and ultimately, tragedy. She was a woman who used her reputation as a tool for survival, a woman caught in the crosshairs of societal change and religious upheaval. As the matron of Pendle, her life and influence continue to reverberate through the annals of English witchcraft history.

Anne, Joan, and Ellen: The Leicester Witches

The English witch trials of the 16th and 17th centuries offer up numerous narratives of superstition, fear, and societal upheaval. The Pendle witch trials are perhaps the most infamous, but they are not the only fascinating case. The trials of Anne Baker, Joan Willimot, and Ellen Greene, collectively known as the Leicester witches, present a tale of cunning women, strange practices, and the power of suggestion.

Anne Baker of Bottesford, Joan Willimot of Goodby, and Ellen Greene of Stathern, were three seemingly innocuous, elderly women from Leicestershire. Their paths crossed not out of choice, but because of the prevailing atmosphere of fear and suspicion of the time. The year was 1619, and King

James I, a fervent believer in the reality of witches and witchcraft, reigned over England.

Anne Baker, a visionary and healer, was the central figure in this tale. She was known for her 'gift of healing', employing prayers and holy water for her remedies. She also claimed the ability to see spirits and was said to have a familiar named Smack, who appeared to her in the form of a grey bird or a dog.

Joan Willimot, a widow, was known as a 'wise woman'. She used 'natural' magic and kept a familiar, Pretty, who appeared to her in the form of a woman and provided her with knowledge of herbs and cures. Joan's practice was an extension of folk traditions and folk wisdom. She functioned as the local healer, providing remedies for ailments that contemporary medicine couldn't cure.

Ellen Greene, on the other hand, was slightly different. While she had a reputation as a healer, there were rumours that she used her powers to harm as well. She was known to use charms, spoken spells, and was said to have a toad named Rutterkin as a familiar.

Their stories intertwined when a local gentleman, William Somers, started experiencing fits and strange visions. Anne Baker was sought to help him, and it was during this course that she accused Joan and Ellen of witchcraft, laying blame on them for William's afflictions.

Investigations into the matter were initiated by a local committee led by Bishop Lewis Bayly. The women were questioned and what followed was a series of confessions that seem unusual to the modern reader. The women didn't deny their practices or their communication with their familiars. Instead, they provided details about them, seemingly oblivious to the consequences.

They were subsequently brought to trial at Leicester Assizes. Anne Baker, who initiated the accusations, was charged with bewitching William Somers, while Joan and Ellen were charged with consorting with evil spirits. Despite their confessions, there was little solid evidence against them. Much of the case relied on the ambiguous nature of their practices and their own confessions.

Remarkably, all three women were found guilty and sentenced to death, a fate that many accused witches met. It was a tragic end to the lives of three women whose only crime, it would seem, was practising traditional healing methods in an era increasingly driven by fear of the unknown and the unseen.

The Leicester witches' trial doesn't just serve as an historical record of injustice. It is also an exploration of a society in flux. Here, in the heart of England, old traditions and new beliefs collided, and those who straddled the line, like Anne, Joan, and Ellen, paid the price.

Their tale reminds us of the significant role women played as keepers of folk traditions and healing practices, roles that became more precarious as society changed. The fear and misunderstanding of these roles, paired with the women's own confessions, shaped their destiny. Their story, though lesser known, is an integral part of the tapestry of England's witch trials, a tapestry woven with threads of fear, suspicion, and a tragic misunderstanding of traditional practices and the women who carried them out.

As we continue our exploration of English witchcraft, the Leicester witches provide a poignant reflection of a society grappling with change. Their story is a testament to the power of fear and suspicion and a sombre reminder of the human cost of ignorance and misunderstanding. In the narrative of English witchcraft, they occupy a unique place, their story one of innocence, vulnerability, and the profound impact of societal beliefs. As such, the Leicester witches and their fate remain an enduring part of England's complex history of witchcraft and magic.

The Witchfinder General: Matthew Hopkins

In the annals of witch-hunting history, few names resonate as chillingly as that of Matthew Hopkins. A self-styled 'Witchfinder General', Hopkins was not a state-appointed officer, but a man whose intense convictions and persuasive rhetoric carved for him a bloody niche in England's history. It was the 17th century, a time of social and religious turmoil, and amidst this backdrop, Hopkins led a campaign of fear and persecution that resulted in the execution of hundreds.

Matthew Hopkins emerged in a period of unrest. The English Civil War was underway, and tensions, fears, and suspicions were rampant. An atmosphere perfect for the rise of a figure like Hopkins, who capitalised on these fears and escalated the witch-hunts to unprecedented levels.

Born around 1620 in Great Wenham, Suffolk, to a Puritan family, Hopkins was a man of relatively humble beginnings. He had some legal training, which likely played a part in his methodical approach to witch-hunting, but there was nothing to suggest the trajectory his life would eventually take.

Hopkins' career as a witchfinder started in March 1644. After hearing a group of women discuss meeting the Devil in Manningtree, Essex, Hopkins took it upon himself to investigate. The subsequent trial and execution of these women was the beginning of a reign of terror that would spread across East Anglia.

His methods were brutal, arbitrary, and exploited the paranoia of the times. Hopkins and his associates, including John Stearne and Mary Phillips, would often 'swim' accused witches – a horrific practice where the suspect was bound and thrown into a body of water. If they floated, they were deemed guilty; if they sank, they were innocent but often drowned in the process.

Another 'test' was the infamous pricking – looking for the Devil's mark. This mark, which was said to be insensitive to pain, was searched for all over the suspect's body. Accused witches were stripped, their bodies pricked with needles. If they didn't bleed, it was considered evidence of witchcraft.

One of the most appalling aspects of Hopkins' methods was the sleep deprivation inflicted on the accused. Deemed as a form of 'gentle torture', it was a loophole to avoid the legal restriction against the use of torture to extract confessions. The accused were kept awake for days, until hallucinations and confessions inevitably followed.

Hopkins was extraordinarily effective. His actions resulted in the execution of an estimated 300 people between 1644 and 1646. This number far exceeded any before in England and was a terrifying manifestation of the hysteria that had gripped society.

But who was Hopkins beneath the horror he orchestrated?

His personal beliefs remain a matter of speculation. Some suggest he was a fervent believer in the devil and witchcraft, driven by religious zeal. Others propose he was an opportunist who saw a chance to exploit societal fear for personal gain.

Whatever the truth, his tactics and campaign were undeniably devastating. The small villages he and his team visited were forever scarred, communities torn apart by accusations, confessions, and subsequent executions. His activities were not without controversy, even at the time. Many, including clergy and legal professionals, questioned his methods and the validity of the confessions he extracted.

His career, as impactful as it was, lasted only two years. In 1646, he published "The Discovery of Witches", a manual justifying his witch-hunting methods. Shortly after, Hopkins retired, citing the toll the witch-hunting was taking on his health. He died in August 1647, leaving behind a legacy of fear, death, and a horrific chapter in England's history.

Today, Matthew Hopkins remains an embodiment of a time when fear and suspicion could be manipulated into a force of devastating cruelty. His actions reflect not just an individual's capacity for harm, but also a society's susceptibility to hysteria and manipulation. His reign, brief as it was, marks one of the darkest periods of witch persecution in English history, a grim testament to the destructive power of fear and a stark reminder of the horrors that can ensue when panic and prejudice are left unchecked.

The Berwick Witches: Mass Hysteria

The year 1590 marked a grim period in the annals of Northumberland. As King James VI of Scotland returned to Scotland from Denmark, a violent storm engulfed his ship, and the monarch's life hung in the balance. The King survived, but the storm's cause was attributed not to natural elements but to a vile supernatural conspiracy involving witchcraft. The subsequent witch-hunt in the small town of Berwick upon Tweed saw eleven people - nine women and two men - fall victim to the mass hysteria surrounding witchcraft.

The storm that stirred the royal angst was not a solitary event. Witches were accused of raising storms to cause the death of nobles and mariners, and King James VI was no exception. The King's obsession with the demonic and supernatural was well known, and his encounter with the storm on his return from Denmark only fuelled his beliefs. He blamed a group of witches from North Berwick in Scotland for causing the tempest, igniting one of the most chilling witch trials known as the North Berwick Witch Trials. But the paranoia didn't stop at the Scottish borders; it trickled down to Berwick upon Tweed in England, leading to the tragic execution of the Berwick Witches.

Berwick, a unique town that changed hands between Scotland and England thirteen times before eventually becoming part of England, found itself embroiled in this panic. A woman named Drembley Thomas was the first to be accused. She was suspected of creating clay figures or poppets, believed to be tools in witchcraft, and using them to curse her enemies. Her accusations started a chain reaction that led to the town's descent into paranoia and fear.

The accused were interrogated, and under duress, they confessed to numerous crimes, including meeting the devil in the church, desecrating the holy space with their rituals, and causing the storm that almost claimed King James's life. This confession validated the King's fears and led to the round-up of more suspected witches.

One of the most infamous confessions came from Agnes Sampson, an elderly woman from North Berwick, who confessed to concocting a potion from the body parts of a cat and a toad, which she and her fellow witches threw into the sea to raise the tempest. While Sampson was tried in Scotland, her confession contributed significantly to the hysteria and paranoia that seeped into Berwick.

The frenzy continued for two years, with trials, confessions, and executions. The confessions extracted from the accused were a product of physical and psychological torture, including sleep deprivation, a method also employed by the notorious Witchfinder General, Matthew Hopkins. Bound, exhausted, and terrified, the victims confessed to ludicrous allegations, fuelling the hysteria further.

The Berwick trials culminated in 1592 with the execution of nine women and two men, all hanged for witchcraft. This event marked a chilling milestone for Berwick and a tragic chapter in the history of witch trials in Britain.

While the Berwick witch trials did not have the numerical scale of the infamous Salem witch trials, they were significant due to their royal connection. They also contributed to King James VI's fear and paranoia, leading him to write the 'Daemonologie', a treatise that endorsed witch hunting and influenced attitudes towards witchcraft in both Scotland and England.

Today, the story of the Berwick witches stands as a potent reminder of the dangers of mass hysteria and the persecution of the marginalised. It's a testament to a dark time when superstition overrode reason, when fear could seal fates, and when the line between good and evil was blurred by paranoia. The tale of the Berwick witches remains etched in history, a chilling legacy of a town caught in the throes of a witch-hunting frenzy.

Mother Shipton: The Prophetess of Knaresborough

Even amidst tales of witchcraft and persecution, stories of prophetic wisdom emerge. Perhaps none is more enduring than the tale of Mother Shipton, the famed prophetess of Knaresborough, England. Known to history as Ursula Southeil, her life and prophetic visions remain a subject of fascination, mystery, and awe.

Ursula Southeil was born to a young woman named Agatha Southeil in the tumultuous year of 1488. Her birth was far from ordinary. Legends whisper of a violent storm that darkened the sky above the cave near the River Nidd where Agatha took shelter, a tale that lent an aura of mystique to Ursula's arrival. Born out of wedlock to a mother of mere 15 years, Ursula's unconventional birth laid the foundations for a life filled with mystery and intrigue.

Her physical appearance, described as 'unique', was the stuff of local folklore. With a large hooked nose, a bent back, and twisted legs, she was an easy target for speculation and fear. This, coupled with her unusual birth circumstances, resulted in a life marred by suspicion and, later, accusations of witchcraft.

Ursula was soon adopted by a local family and, at 24, married Toby Shipton, a carpenter from Shipton. From then on, she was known as Mother Shipton. Although the couple had no children, Mother Shipton was known for her affinity towards the children of Knaresborough, often sharing her visions and prophecies with them.

The origins of her prophetic visions remain shrouded in mystery. There are tales of Ursula hearing voices in her childhood, but it wasn't until her adulthood that her true potential as a prophetess unfolded. She was known for predicting local events, from fires to famines, with alarming accuracy. Word of her prophetic abilities spread, and she was both feared and revered for her prescience.

The fame of Mother Shipton reached its zenith posthumously when her prophecies were published in 1641. This collection of prophecies covered a wide range of subjects, from personal affairs to political events, spanning decades after her death. What was extraordinary was the uncanny accuracy of these predictions. The most famous among these was her prediction of the dissolution of the monasteries by Henry VIII, the Great Fire of London in 1666, and even the advent of modern technology.

One of her most famous lines of prophecy reads: "Carriages without horses shall go, And accidents fill the world with woe. Around the world, thoughts shall fly In the twinkling of an eye." Many have interpreted this as a reference to cars, aeroplanes, and the internet, technologies that would have been unimaginable in the 16th century.

Despite her clear foresight, Mother Shipton's life was not devoid of controversy. Accusations of witchcraft followed her, fueled by her physical appearance, her strange birth, and her extraordinary gift. Yet, there is no record of her facing the persecution common to many accused witches of her time. Instead, her influence continued to grow, and her prophecies became the subject of numerous publications and interpretations over centuries.

The legacy of Mother Shipton endures, much like the petrifying well near her birthplace, which turns objects into stone, an appropriate symbol of the lasting impact of this remarkable woman. Despite numerous attempts to debunk her prophecies, Mother Shipton remains a figure of enduring intrigue, a woman who was both of her time and beyond it.

Today, the tale of Mother Shipton continues to captivate the imaginations of those who hear it, encapsulating the paradoxes of a world where wisdom and persecution, fear and reverence, and the human and the supernatural intertwined. Through Mother Shipton, we glimpse a world where the prophecy of a 'witch' could predict the course of kingdoms, the fate of technologies yet unborn, and the future of humanity itself. Ursula Southeil, the Prophetess of

Knaresborough, serves as a compelling testament to the intriguing tapestry of England's relationship with witchcraft and prophecy.

Agnes Waterhouse: The First Witch of Chelmsford

In the chronicles of witchcraft in England, few stories startle and fascinate like the tale of Agnes Waterhouse, one of the first women to be executed for witchcraft in the country. Her story echoes the fears, beliefs, and legal developments of her time, shaping our understanding of the witch trials that swept through England in the 16th and 17th centuries.

Born in the mid-15th century, Agnes Waterhouse lived most of her life in the small town of Hatfield Peverel, near Chelmsford, Essex. She was widowed and lived with her daughter, Joan, and her granddaughter, also named Joan. Their household was a regular one by most accounts, with little to suggest the dramatic turn their lives would take.

The Waterhouse's story intersects with that of another family, the Laminates. The widowed Elizabeth Francis, a resident of Hatfield Peverel, was suspected of witchcraft. She allegedly owned a white spotted cat named Sathan, inherited from her grandmother, who used it to cast spells and curses. Elizabeth was Agnes's sister.

The year 1566 marked a turning point for both the Waterhouse and the Francis families. Elizabeth was accused of witchcraft by her neighbours. Her charges stemmed from a wide array of misfortunes suffered by the townsfolk – failed crops, sick cattle, and even the death of an infant, all attributed to Elizabeth's supposed sorcery.

Elizabeth was arrested, and during her questioning, she confessed to her crimes and revealed an unexpected detail. She claimed to have given Sathan, her magical cat, to Agnes Waterhouse. Elizabeth's confession dragged Agnes, her daughter, and her granddaughter into the vortex of the witch trials.

Agnes's trial was a significant event, one of the first major witch trials following the 1563 passage of "An Act Against Conjurations, Enchantments, and Witchcrafts." This Act made witchcraft a secular crime, punishable by death, forever altering the course of such accusations in England.

The trial transcripts provide a startling glimpse into the proceedings. Agnes was accused of using her cat, Sathan, to carry out malicious acts. She allegedly caused the death of a man named William Fynne and tormented another man, causing him continuous pain. Furthermore, she confessed to using Sathan to kill her livestock when they failed to provide enough milk.

Perhaps the most chilling part of the trial was Agnes's confession. She spoke calmly and clearly, showing no remorse or fear, only an eerily detached resignation to her fate. She admitted to practising witchcraft, using her cat to harm her neighbours, and even teaching her daughter and granddaughter to do the same.

However, the accusations didn't stop at causing physical

harm. Agnes was also charged with the most serious crime a witch could commit - making a pact with the devil. She admitted that she had nurtured a relationship with the devil for over 15 years, stating that she often let him suck blood from her body.

The fate of Agnes Waterhouse was sealed. She was found guilty and sentenced to death by hanging, making her one of the first recorded women to be executed for witchcraft in England. Elizabeth Francis was also found guilty but was given a year of imprisonment and four appearances in the pillory. Agnes's daughter Joan was acquitted due to lack of evidence.

The story of Agnes Waterhouse forces us to reckon with a time when fear and superstition held a formidable grip over the collective consciousness. It reveals the tragic consequences when panic, fear, and law merge, leading to the senseless persecution of individuals. As we explore the labyrinth of witch trials in England, Agnes Waterhouse's tale stands out, a chilling testament to the perils of ignorance, fear, and the misuse of law, casting a long, dark shadow over England's history.

The St Osyth Witches: The Accursed Town

Situated in the County of Essex, the peaceful coastal village of St Osyth might deceive any casual visitor with its tranquil landscapes and quaint architecture. However, peel back the serene veneer, and you'll uncover a turbulent past, steeped in tales of witchcraft and trials that form a substantial part of England's paranormal history.

The 16th and 17th centuries were a time when the fear of witchcraft and the supernatural was pervasive in England, and St Osyth was not spared. The village found itself at the centre of numerous witch trials, resulting in the execution of many innocent women. The chilling tales of these accused witches, their trials, and the hysteria that enveloped the village during these years are the subjects of this chapter.

The story of witchcraft in St Osyth primarily revolves around two significant trials that occurred in 1582 and 1645. These trials and the people involved exemplify the paranoia and the tragically flawed justice system of the time.

In 1582, two women, Ursula Kemp and Elizabeth Bennet, found themselves in the unenviable position of being accused of witchcraft. Ursula was a well-known midwife in the village, and Elizabeth was a local woman with a rather quarrelsome reputation. They were charged based on a broad range of accusations, from causing illness and death to causing livestock to produce less milk.

Interestingly, it was a local man, Thomas Rabbet, who set the wheels of accusation in motion. Thomas's son had fallen ill, and he firmly believed that Ursula Kemp, his neighbour, was to blame. He claimed that after a dispute, Ursula had cursed his son, leading to his illness. His beliefs found resonance in a community already on edge due to the growing fear of witchcraft across England.

The trial transcripts reveal the severity of the accusations made against Ursula and Elizabeth. They were accused of summoning spirits, casting spells, and consorting with the devil. During the trial, under immense pressure, Ursula confessed to owning four familiars that she claimed helped her in her nefarious activities. Elizabeth, too, confessed, although it was likely the result of coercion and fear.

Ursula Kemp and Elizabeth Bennet were found guilty of witchcraft and hanged, marking the first significant witch trial in St Osyth. However, this was just the beginning. The stage was set for an even larger trial that would again plunge St Osyth into a frenzy of witch hunting.

Fast forward to 1645, and St Osyth found itself in the grip of another wave of witch hysteria, fuelled by the infamous Witchfinder General, Matthew Hopkins. This time, the scale of accusations was even more significant. In what came to be known as the St Osyth Witch Hunt, fourteen women were accused of witchcraft. The charges were familiar –

causing sickness, death, and having dealings with the devil.

Despite the lack of solid evidence, and the fact that many confessions were extracted under torture, six of the fourteen women were found guilty and hanged. These events marked one of the most extensive single witch hunts in English history, solidifying St Osyth's dark reputation in the annals of witchcraft.

The legacy of the witch trials continues to cast a long shadow over St Osyth. The village's history is inextricably linked with these events, adding a layer of eerie fascination to its peaceful facades. The stories of the St Osyth witches are not only tales of persecution but also a testament to the dangerous power of fear and hysteria that can consume communities.

These tales serve as a reminder of a dark period in English history, where superstition overruled reason, fear fuelled the pursuit of justice, and the innocent paid the ultimate price. As we revisit these stories, let them serve as both a reflection on our past and a cautionary tale for our future.

Elizabeth Sawyer: The Witch of Edmonton

Elizabeth Sawyer, an enigmatic figure of the early 17th century, holds a unique position within the tapestry of England's witch trials. Unlike many accused witches, her story didn't merely end with her trial and execution. Instead, it transcended time and mediums, eventually being adapted into a renowned Jacobean play, "The Witch of Edmonton," forever immortalising her narrative.

Born in the small community of Edmonton, now part of modern-day London, Elizabeth was an everyday woman who, by a cruel twist of fate, became embroiled in a witchcraft scandal that ended her life and subsequently defined her legacy. This chapter explores her story, the societal factors that contributed to her downfall, and how her narrative became a source of inspiration for one of the most enduring plays of Jacobean theatre.

Elizabeth Sawyer lived an unremarkable life as a wife and a mother, surviving through the bitter winters and bountiful summers of the 17th century. By most accounts, she was an ill-favoured, impoverished woman, noted for her harsh language and irascible nature. However, it was these same characteristics that ultimately led her neighbours to suspect her of witchcraft.

The sequence of events leading to Elizabeth's downfall began with a trivial incident - an altercation with her neighbour, Agnes Ratcliffe, over some trivial matter. This dispute was the spark that lit the fuse of suspicion. Following this argument, Ratcliffe's pig suddenly died, leading her to openly accuse Elizabeth of bewitching the animal.

As word of the incident spread throughout the community, an already prevalent fear of witchcraft took hold, and Elizabeth, with her notorious temper and solitary lifestyle, became the prime suspect. Soon, more villagers came forward with tales of dead livestock, mysterious ailments, and strange occurrences, all conveniently traced back to Elizabeth.

The local Justice of the Peace, Henry Goodcole, caught wind of these allegations and saw it as his divine duty to investigate. Goodcole was a fervent believer in witchcraft, and his probing inquiries further fanned the flames of suspicion. It was during one of his interrogations that Elizabeth, possibly under duress, confessed to having a familiar in the form of a dog named Tom.

Elizabeth's trial in 1621 was a foregone conclusion. Despite the lack of solid evidence, her confession, likely obtained under pressure, sealed her fate. She was convicted of witchcraft and hanged on April 19th, 1621, forever branded as the Witch of Edmonton.

While the conclusion of Elizabeth's life was tragic, it was the posthumous depiction of her story that truly etched her name into history. "The Witch of Edmonton," a play written by William Rowley, Thomas Dekker, and John Ford, took inspiration from her life. Published a year after Elizabeth's execution, the play presented a nuanced exploration of her story, delving into themes of social ostracism, ignorance, and the consequences of unfounded hysteria.

The play's depiction of Elizabeth Sawyer is as intriguing as it is tragic. She is shown as a lonely, marginalised figure, driven to despair by the unjust suspicions and cruel treatment of her neighbours. Despite her dark pact with the devil, portrayed in the form of her dog, Tom, the play elicits a degree of sympathy for Elizabeth. The playwrights skillfully highlight the societal conditions and prejudices that led her to her fatal predicament, offering a stark critique of contemporary attitudes towards witchcraft.

"The Witch of Edmonton" stood out amidst other Jacobean witchcraft plays due to its grounding in reality. While many other plays leaned heavily into fantastical elements, this one sought to represent the actual social dynamics and injustices that facilitated witch-hunts. Over the years, the play has continued to be studied and performed, keeping

Elizabeth Sawyer's story alive well into the 21st century.

Elizabeth Sawyer's story is a poignant testament to the dangerous intersection of societal prejudice, fear, and ignorance. It's a grim reminder of a time when a woman's fate could be sealed by a neighbour's suspicion, a harsh word spoken in anger, or even the untimely death of livestock. As we delve deeper into England's history of witch trials, her story offers a lens to view the human cost of these tragic events.

In Elizabeth's narrative, we see not just a tale of witchcraft, but also a complex, compelling exploration of societal dynamics, fear, and injustice. Her life, execution, and the subsequent artistic portrayal provide an invaluable perspective on the realities of witch trials in 17th century England. And so, through the retelling of her story, we aim to learn from our past and strive towards a more understanding and empathetic society.

The Witches of Warboys

The chilling tale of the Witches of Warboys, often overshadowed by the more notorious witch trials such as those in Pendle and Salem, nevertheless deserves its place in the annals of witchcraft history. Not only does it depict the rampant hysteria and susceptibility to supernatural beliefs prevalent in 16th century England, but it also presents one of the earliest legal cases of witchcraft that culminated in the execution of an entire family. At the heart of this story is the figure of Alice Samuel and her family, accused of bewitching the well-connected Throckmorton family.

Set in the quiet village of Warboys, located in Huntingdonshire, England, the story begins in 1589. The Throckmorton family, wealthy and influential, were leading figures in their community. Their lives of relative peace were disrupted when their eldest daughter, Jane Throckmorton, began experiencing strange fits and convulsions.

The physicians of the time, bereft of any medical explanation for Jane's condition, suggested that the cause might be supernatural. What started with Jane soon spread to her four younger sisters, who also began exhibiting similar symptoms. The young girls claimed to see visions of a spectre and uttered incoherent statements, a phenomenon that drew attention and generated fear within their close-knit community.

Amidst the growing chaos, Jane accused Alice Samuel, a humble, middle-aged woman of the village, of bewitching her. The accusation was based on an encounter where Alice had strangely muttered about the fine furs the Throckmorton girls were wearing, an incident Jane interpreted as an evil spell. As the girls' afflictions continued and even intensified, the blame solidified on Alice.

Alice Samuel, her husband John, and their daughter Agnes found themselves the targets of community outrage and fear. They faced relentless interrogations and were even brought into the Throckmorton household in an attempt to prove their guilt. The girls' symptoms would apparently cease in Alice's presence, only to return with increased ferocity once she left. Alice, under immense pressure, eventually confessed to witchcraft, although she later retracted her statement, asserting that it had been coerced.

However, Alice's confession set irreversible events in motion. The Samuels were brought before the courts in 1593. Even though the evidence against them was purely circumstantial and largely based on the spectral visions of the Throckmorton girls, it proved compelling in the superstitious climate of the time. The court found the Samuels guilty of witchcraft, and they were subsequently executed in April 1593.

The Warboys witch trial highlights the ease with which suspicion and paranoia can spread in a close-knit community. Alice Samuel, a seemingly ordinary woman, was transformed into a figure of terror based on ambiguous evidence and the hearsay of a few impressionable children. The lack of substantial proof and the willingness of the courts to accept spectral evidence reflect the heightened fear and lack of understanding of the time.

Furthermore, the case was instrumental in shaping the legal proceedings of future witch trials in England. The involvement of the Throckmorton family, who were related by marriage to the influential Cromwell family, brought the case to the attention of the nobility. It's believed that the visibility of the Warboys case, due to the Throckmortons' status, contributed to King James I's interest in witchcraft, which later resulted in the passage of the Witchcraft Act of 1604.

The case of the Witches of Warboys holds a mirror to a time of superstition and misunderstanding. It is a sobering reminder of how fear can drive a community to hysteria and the tragic consequences of such fear when coupled with a legal system willing to entertain spectral evidence. As we continue to explore the history of witches in England, cases like Warboys serve as stark reminders of the social and judicial milieu that fueled the persecution of alleged witches, causing the destruction of lives based on fear rather than fact.

Cunning Folk and Pellers: The Other Side of the Coin

In our exploration of the annals of English witchcraft, we have encountered tales of suspicion, persecution, and sorrow. Often, these stories spotlight the vulnerable, the marginalised, and the misunderstood. But to understand the complete picture of witchcraft in England, we must also turn our gaze to a different but closely related phenomenon - the practice of folk magic by cunning folk and pellers, who, despite playing a crucial role in their communities, were sometimes mistaken for witches and paid the price for their invaluable services.

Cunning folk, also known as wise men or wise women, were commonplace in England from the 15th century to the early 20th century. They were individuals believed to possess supernatural abilities used for healing, fortune-telling, and protection against malevolent witchcraft. In a time when professional medical help was scarce, costly, and often ineffective, cunning folk served as the community's primary caregivers, counsellors, and protectors.

Similar to cunning folk were pellers. These practitioners of folk magic were specialised in 'pellings' or spells, which they used for various purposes, from love charms to protective wards against evil spirits. While their practices overlapped with those of cunning folk, pellers were often more associated with the magical rather than the healing aspects of folk tradition.

The world of cunning folk and pellers was shrouded in mystery and intrigue. They were believed to have acquired their knowledge and skills through family inheritance, apprenticeships, or even supernatural means such as dreams and divine encounters. They would carry out their practices in secrecy, usually in their homes or secluded places, using a range of tools and materials, from herbs and crystals to written charms known as 'bills'.

Despite the essential services they provided, cunning folk and pellers were not immune to the social and religious scrutiny that bore down heavily on those associated with the supernatural. Their practices, though predominantly benign or benevolent, could be seen as transgressive, disrupting the church's authority and the established social order. This could often lead to their being mistaken for witches, especially during periods of heightened witch panic.

The Church, while initially tolerant of these practitioners due to their protective function against witchcraft, started to perceive them as a threat to religious orthodoxy. The belief in witchcraft and the power of cunning folk and pellers to counteract it was seen as superstition that undermined the Church's teachings. By the late 16th century, cunning folk were increasingly targeted by witchcraft laws, marking a shift in perception from community protectors to potential malefactors.

Despite the risks, cunning folk and pellers continued to practise and were sought out by people from all walks of life, from peasant to nobleman. This endurance attests to their social importance and the crucial role they played in addressing the psychological and emotional needs of the community. They functioned as an outlet for fears, anxieties, and hopes in a world fraught with uncertainty, disease, and misfortune.

The study of cunning folk and pellers offers us an intriguing and insightful look into the rich tapestry of magic, belief, and superstition that characterised early modern England. While on one side, we see the vilification and persecution of alleged witches, on the other, we find these practitioners of folk magic offering their services, often risking their lives, in response to the needs and beliefs of their time.

Cunning folk and pellers were not mere footnotes in the chronicle of English witchcraft. They were central figures who showcased the multifaceted nature of magical belief in England, spanning the spectrum from feared witchcraft to beneficial magic. Their existence and persistence serve as a reminder of the complexity of the past and the nuanced ways in which beliefs about magic have influenced societal relations, religious practices, and legal frameworks.

In the chapters to come, as we continue our journey into the world of English witchcraft, we will keep in mind these practitioners of benevolent magic. Their stories underline the paradox of a society that both feared and sought out the supernatural, a tension that would play out tragically in the lives of the alleged witches we encounter. Yet, through understanding this tension, we gain a more complete and empathetic view of a time marked by both fear and fascination with the world of the unseen.

Elizabeth Clarke: Hopkins' First Victim

A moonless night blanketed the small village of Manningtree, Essex, in the early spring of 1645. There, within the confines of a humble, thatched dwelling, resided Elizabeth Clarke, a one-legged widow of an insignificant labourer. In her late eighties, with only a crutch for support and a pet cat for company, Elizabeth was far from the image of a terrifying witch that folklore often depicted. Yet, her name would soon be forever linked to witchcraft, not because of her supernatural prowess but her status as the first victim of the self-styled Witchfinder General, Matthew Hopkins.

The story of Elizabeth Clarke, like the tales of many accused witches in England, is one steeped in social, economic, and cultural factors that transcend mere superstition. For Elizabeth, these factors—her physical disability, gender, widowhood, and impoverishment—collectively cast her into the tragic role of a scapegoat, bearing the brunt of communal anxieties and an ambitious man's ruthless drive for power.

Elizabeth Clarke's story begins long before her fateful encounter with Hopkins. Having lost her husband and children, Elizabeth lived alone on the fringes of society, existing on parish relief and the occasional goodwill of her neighbours. Her lack of family support and visible physical impairment made her a conspicuous figure, an outsider in the eyes of the Manningtree community.

Her vulnerability was further exacerbated by the widespread belief that physical disability was a sign of God's displeasure or the devil's mark, indicating a pact with the forces of evil. Such views, coupled with Elizabeth's dependence on the community, laid fertile ground for rumours and accusations to take root and flourish.

The instigator of these rumours was none other than Matthew Hopkins, a man who would soon earn notoriety as England's most prolific witch-hunter. A newcomer to Manningtree, Hopkins, with his zealous pursuit of witches, found a perfect target in Elizabeth. The reasons behind Hopkins' focus on witch-hunting are speculated to have been both personal and pecuniary. For Hopkins, witch-hunting offered a path to social elevation and financial gain, benefits that he pursued with fervour.

With the claim of having heard Elizabeth speak blasphemous words against God, Hopkins formally accused her of witchcraft. Thus, Elizabeth became the first quarry of Hopkins' grim witch-hunting campaign. Arrested and brought to Colchester Castle, Elizabeth was subjected to a gruelling and inhumane interrogation that would set a grim precedent for Hopkins' future victims.

The trials of the time were less an examination of evidence and more a theatre of the absurd, with the fate of the accused hanging on ludicrous tests and confessions often extracted under duress. In Elizabeth's case, she was subjected to a 'witch's watch', a torturous practice wherein the accused was stripped naked and watched continuously by a team of watchers for signs of her familiars.

After being kept awake for three nights, a delirious and exhausted Elizabeth reportedly confessed to having familiars. These included a greyhound, a black rabbit, a polecat, and even her pet cat, named Holt. Each familiar, she said, had promised to perform wicked deeds on her behalf, a confession that essentially sealed her fate.

Following her confession, Elizabeth was put on trial at Chelmsford Assizes in July 1645, one among the many accused witches. Her purported confessions, used as damning evidence against her, led to her conviction and execution by hanging. Thus ended the life of Elizabeth Clarke, a life taken by a potent mix of societal prejudice, superstition, and one man's ruthless ambition.

Elizabeth's tragic story serves as a stark reminder of the myriad ways societal prejudices can fuel fear, paranoia, and cruelty. It also paints a chilling picture of the ease with which fear can be manipulated by those seeking power and gain.

As we delve deeper into the labyrinth of England's witch-hunting history, we shall continue to bear witness to such stories, reminders of the human cost of fear and the power dynamics that exploit it. Elizabeth Clarke, the first victim of Matthew Hopkins' campaign, is but one name among many, each tale echoing the perils of a society gripped by witch mania.

Daemonologie: Witchcraft from a Royal Perspective

James I of England and VI of Scotland was not only a monarch but a scholar with a keen interest in theology, philosophy, and the supernatural. His fascination with the latter, particularly with witchcraft, would define his reign and leave a lasting impact on how witchcraft was perceived and prosecuted in England. This chapter takes us to the heart of the royal court in the early 17th century, unravelling the beliefs and policies of King James and their influence on the witch trials of the time.

Born in 1566, James inherited the throne of Scotland as an infant. He grew up in a kingdom steeped in superstition, with widespread belief in witchcraft and the demonic. His early exposure to such beliefs, particularly to the idea of witches as servants of the Devil intent on causing harm, left an indelible mark on the young monarch's mind.

James' interest in witchcraft deepened following his marriage to Anne of Denmark in 1589. On their return voyage to Scotland, the royal couple encountered violent storms that nearly claimed their lives. These storms were later attributed to witchcraft, leading to the infamous North Berwick witch trials where several people were prosecuted and executed.

This personal encounter with the supposed powers of witchcraft solidified James' belief in its reality and malevolence. His response was scholarly as much as it was practical: he embarked on an intellectual exploration of witchcraft, resulting in the publication of "Daemonologie" in 1597. This treatise, written in the form of a dialogue, examined various aspects of witchcraft and the demonic. James firmly advocated the existence of witches, their malefic pacts with the Devil, and the necessity of their prosecution.

When James ascended to the English throne in 1603, he brought with him these entrenched beliefs. However, he found the English approach to witchcraft quite different from the Scottish one. The legal treatment of witchcraft in England was less severe, the scepticism towards witch accusations more widespread.

Undeterred by these differences, James set about influencing English attitudes and laws concerning witchcraft. In 1604, within a year of his ascension, the Witchcraft Act was passed. This act amplified the seriousness of witchcraft as a crime, making not only the practice of malefic witchcraft a capital offence but even the mere attempt or intention to perform such acts.

James' belief in the reality and malevolence of witchcraft was perhaps most clearly demonstrated in his personal involvement in witch trials. The most notable of these was the case of Anne Gunter in 1604, who accused three women of bewitching her. James ordered a rigorous investigation, personally examining Anne and her alleged tormentors. Though the case was ultimately exposed as a hoax, it highlighted James' personal commitment to rooting out witchcraft.

The King's beliefs permeated the judiciary as well. His treatise, "Daemonologie," was often used as a guide in witch trials, and his laws facilitated more stringent prosecution of accused witches. Consequently, there was a significant rise in the number of witch trials and executions during James' reign.

Yet, it's important to note that James' approach to witchcraft was not uniformly dogmatic. As his reign progressed, he displayed an increasing scepticism towards some witchcraft accusations, recognizing the possibility of false allegations and the misuse of witchcraft fears. This led to a certain degree of ambivalence in later years, which in turn contributed to a gradual decrease in witch trials and executions.

The reign of James I marked a crucial period in the history of witchcraft in England. His personal beliefs, combined with his position as a monarch, allowed him to shape societal and legal attitudes towards witchcraft in significant ways. Whether his influence exacerbated the persecution of alleged witches or advanced the understanding of witchcraft as a socio-cultural phenomenon is a question that invites further contemplation. As we navigate through the labyrinthine corridors of England's witch-hunting history, the shadow of King James I looms large, reminding us of the complex and often contradictory nature of witchcraft beliefs and their deadly implications.

The Case of Eleanor Cobham: Witchcraft in the Royal Court

In the annals of England's illustrious history, the royal court has seen more than its fair share of intrigues, scandals, and nefarious plots. Yet few episodes have been as strange and ominous as the case of Eleanor Cobham, Duchess of Gloucester, whose association with witchcraft led to one of the earliest recorded witch trials in the country.

Eleanor Cobham was born into a family of minor gentry, but her beauty and charm soon attracted the attention of the powerful Humphrey, Duke of Gloucester. Humphrey was a man of significant influence in the court, being the younger brother of King Henry V and later the Lord Protector during the infancy of King Henry VI. Eleanor, following a scandalous affair and a quiet wedding, found herself catapulted to the upper echelons of the English aristocracy.

The royal court was an arena of high stakes and fierce competition, and Eleanor's status as a commoner-turned-duchess made her a target for the nobility who believed that she was overstepping her rank. However, it was not just the machinations of her aristocratic enemies that would lead to her downfall; it was her own ambitions and her attempts to secure her future by supernatural means.

The scandal unfolded in 1441 when an astrologer named Roger Bolingbroke, known to be an associate of Eleanor, was arrested and brought before the King's Council. Upon questioning, Bolingbroke confessed to using astrological divinations to predict the death of King Henry VI – an act considered high treason. However, the most shocking revelation was that Bolingbroke claimed he was acting under the instructions of Eleanor Cobham herself.

Eleanor, it appeared, had sought out Bolingbroke to forecast her chances of becoming queen. Intriguingly, the accusations did not stop at mere astrological divinations.

Bolingbroke claimed that Eleanor had also sought the assistance of Margery Jourdemayne, a woman widely known as the 'Witch of Eye' for her knowledge of potions and spells. The alleged conspiracy was that Eleanor had employed Jourdemayne to concoct potions and love philtres to help her maintain her hold on the Duke of Gloucester and secure her ascension to the throne.

These were grave allegations. Engaging in sorcery was viewed as a direct affront to the Church and God's divine order, and attempting to predict or manipulate the death of the King was treasonous. Amid the uproar that followed, Eleanor was arrested and subjected to a public trial that was both a legal proceeding and a spectacle meant to discourage similar transgressions.

In her trial, Eleanor fervently denied the accusations of treason but admitted to obtaining potions from Jourdemayne. She claimed that these were not to manipulate the King or her husband but to help her conceive a child. Nevertheless, the admission was damning. The court, swayed by Bolingbroke's confession and

Eleanor's own admission, found her guilty.

The consequences were severe. Eleanor was made to do public penance, divorced from her husband, and condemned to life imprisonment. Bolingbroke was hanged, drawn, and quartered, while Jourdemayne was burnt at the stake - a grim reminder of the Church's stance on witchcraft.

The case of Eleanor Cobham is significant for several reasons. It demonstrates the severity of the penalties for witchcraft, even for those of high status. It shows the complex interplay between power, ambition, and supernatural beliefs in the royal court, and the use of witchcraft accusations as a tool for political manoeuvring.

Eleanor's story, from her meteoric rise to her tragic downfall, offers a fascinating glimpse into the socio-political climate of 15th-century England. It also foreshadows the storm of witch-hunts that would sweep the country in the centuries to come. Yet, amidst the intrigue and the scandal, Eleanor Cobham, the Duchess of Gloucester, remains a poignant figure, her fate a testament to the dangerous allure of power and the shadowy realm of the supernatural.

The Witches of Belvoir: A Noble Family's Curse

In the verdant, rolling hills of Leicestershire, Belvoir Castle stands as a towering monument to the grandeur of England's noble past. Its stone walls and turreted battlements harbour centuries of history, including an unsettling episode that casts a dark shadow over its otherwise illustrious past. This chapter recounts the tragic tale of the Witches of Belvoir, three women ensnared in a web of supernatural suspicion that led to their downfall.

In the early 17th century, Belvoir Castle was the stately home of the Manners family, headed by the Earl of Rutland, Francis Manners. The family was well-respected and had enjoyed considerable favour from King James I. However, their seemingly idyllic existence was marred by an inexplicable tragedy. Both of the Earl's sons and heirs, Henry and Francis, met untimely deaths. The boys' unexpected demise sent shockwaves through the aristocracy and sent the grieving Earl on a desperate quest for answers.

The cause of the young heirs' deaths remained elusive until attention turned to Joan Flower and her daughters, Margaret and Philippa. The Flower women were servants at Belvoir Castle but were dismissed due to accusations of theft. In a time of increasing superstition and fear of the supernatural, it didn't take long for murmurs of witchcraft to begin.

Rumours suggested that the Flower women had taken their dismissal poorly, nursing a grudge against the Earl and his family. The local populace whispered that Joan and her daughters had turned to dark forces to exact their revenge. The nature of the children's deaths, which involved sudden illness and a rapid decline, fuelled these suspicions.

Borne by a wave of panic and suspicion, the women were

arrested and subjected to rigorous interrogation. What followed was a confession that sent ripples of dread throughout the kingdom. Joan Flower, the matriarch, rejected the communion bread, a sure sign of guilt in the witch trials. The act led to her subsequent death in prison, which was viewed as an admission of her guilt.

Her daughters, Margaret and Philippa, displayed a more alarming admission of guilt. Under the intense pressure of the trial, they confessed to stealing the young Lords' gloves and giving them to their mother, who, using spells and incantations, had invoked evil spirits to cause the boys' deaths. Further, they claimed to have consorted with familiar spirits, a common allegation in witch trials of the time.

The confessions, likely procured under duress, sealed the women's fates. Margaret and Philippa were convicted of witchcraft and hanged at Lincoln Castle in 1619. The trial and execution of the Flower women were among the most high-profile witch cases in Jacobean England and highlighted the widespread belief in witchcraft, even among the nobility.

The case of the Witches of Belvoir illustrates the extent to which fear of the supernatural permeated all levels of society. Even the noble families, typically insulated by their wealth and status, were not immune to the hysteria surrounding witchcraft. The Earl of Rutland's decision to attribute his sons' deaths to witchcraft, as opposed to natural causes, shows a profound belief in, and fear of, the power of witches.

However, the story also illustrates the vulnerability of women in a society gripped by paranoia. Joan, Margaret, and Philippa Flower, likely victims of societal scapegoating, found themselves facing the full brunt of the law and a fearful populace.

Finally, it's worth noting the part that socio-economic tensions played in the case. The Flower women, lower-class servants dismissed under a cloud of disgrace, were convenient targets for a noble family struck by sudden and inexplicable tragedy. Their downfall served as a stark warning to others about the dangers of crossing those more powerful.

The Witches of Belvoir, a tale steeped in fear, tragedy, and injustice, adds another layer of complexity to the history of witchcraft in England. It speaks to the far-reaching power of superstition and the ease with which fear can translate into fatal accusations. As we delve deeper into England's history of witchcraft, we continue to uncover tales that reflect not only on the supernatural beliefs of the past but also on the socio-political tensions of the era.

Margaret Jourdemayne: The Witch of Eye Next Westminster

The annals of English witchcraft bristle with tales of ordinary women dragged into extraordinary circumstances, their lives abruptly derailed by accusations of consorting with the devil and harnessing sinister powers. But few stories resonate with the high drama of politics, scandal, and treachery that characterised the life of Margaret Jourdemayne, commonly known as the Witch of Eye Next Westminster.

Margaret Jourdemayne, an ostensibly simple woman living near Westminster, led a life fraught with infamy and danger in 15th-century England, a tumultuous era marked by political conspiracies, royal rivalries, and widespread belief in witchcraft. She was a reputed wise woman, well-versed in the use of medicinal herbs and potions, and was frequently sought by people seeking help with various ailments, childbearing issues, and even fortune-telling.

However, Margaret's skills extended beyond the realm of the ordinary. She was infamous for her supposed ability to invoke spirits and foresee the future. These mystical traits, coupled with her knack for herbalism, earned her the title of 'witch' among the locals. Margaret, despite her notorious reputation, was highly sought after, her clients including individuals from all social strata, from the poorest commoners to influential nobles.

The first witchcraft accusation against Margaret occurred in 1419 when she was charged with causing the death of a man through her magical practices. However, she managed to escape execution, likely through influential connections. Margaret was merely given a life sentence in the Church's prison. Her relatively light sentence, in an era when witchcraft was usually a capital offence, was considered an extraordinary exception, providing a glimpse into the respect and fear that her powers commanded.

However, Margaret's most notorious involvement was yet to come. Following her release from prison, she found herself entwined in a plot that sent shockwaves through the highest echelons of the English monarchy. The year was 1441, and the reign of the young King Henry VI was marked by political uncertainty and turmoil. The most significant event was the "Southwark Plot", a conspiracy to end the king's life and influence the line of succession.

The central figures in this plot were Eleanor, Duchess of Gloucester, wife of the powerful Humphrey, Duke of Gloucester and Lord Protector of England, and her accomplices, Roger Bolingbroke, a renowned astrologer, and Thomas Southwell, a priest. They sought Margaret's expertise in the dark arts to predict and manipulate the king's life.

The plot unfolded with Bolingbroke performing a series of astrological readings to determine the king's lifespan. At the same time, Southwell and the Duchess turned to Margaret, hoping to utilise her alleged powers to affect the king's life. However, their schemes came to light when a servant of the Duke of Gloucester discovered their actions.

Once exposed, Margaret, along with Bolingbroke and Southwell, was arrested and tried for high treason. Their trial was one of the most sensational events of the time, attracting significant public and noble attention. The scandal was further amplified due to the involvement of the Duchess of Gloucester, a high-ranking noblewoman.

Margaret's second brush with the law ended in a harsher verdict than her first. Found guilty of treason and witchcraft, she was sentenced to death by burning, a sentence explicitly reserved for the most severe crimes against the Crown and Church. Margaret Jourdemayne was executed at Smithfield in London, her life ending in a blaze that signified the severity of her crimes.

In the context of English witchcraft, the tale of Margaret Jourdemayne is unique and telling. Not only does it highlight the pervasive belief in magic and the supernatural among all social classes, but it also illustrates how accusations of witchcraft could serve as political tools. Margaret's execution for high treason underscored the severity of her involvement in a conspiracy against the king. However, it is equally likely that her reputation as a witch was used to magnify the perceived threat and further vilify those involved in the plot.

Despite her tragic end, Margaret Jourdemayne left a lasting impression on the history of English witchcraft. The Witch of Eye Next Westminster, an ordinary woman enmeshed in extraordinary circumstances, continues to intrigue historians and enthusiasts, her story serving as a potent reminder of the complex intersection of power, belief, and fear in 15th-century England.

The Mompesson Haunting: Witchcraft or Ghost Story?

The vivid history of English witchcraft and folklore is speckled with accounts of spectral happenings, spectres, and phantoms. However, few instances of supposed supernatural activity can match the profound eeriness and lasting mystery of the events that unfolded in the Mompesson household in the late 17th century. Unveiled against a backdrop of prevailing belief in witchcraft and the supernatural, the Mompesson haunting remains a puzzling blend of witchcraft and a ghost story, its precise origins and causes cloaked in layers of ambiguity and conjecture.

Our narrative unfolds in the year 1661, in the picturesque town of Tedworth (now Tidworth) in Wiltshire, England. The central characters in this chilling drama are the

Mompesson family - John Mompesson, a local magistrate, his wife, and their children. The family lived in a substantial, comfortable house, indicative of their respectable status in the local community.

The eerie chain of events began with an incident of seemingly little consequence. John Mompesson, in his role as a magistrate, had confiscated a drum from a vagrant named William Drury, who was charged with causing a public nuisance. This seemingly mundane act of local law enforcement would inadvertently trigger a sequence of events that would lead the Mompesson household into a terrifying ordeal.

Shortly after Drury's drum was seized, strange occurrences began to plague the Mompesson household. The family started to hear inexplicable knocking and drumming sounds echoing through their home in the dead of night, a phenomenon that would continue for months. The sounds varied from soft taps to loud, violent bangs that seemed to reverberate from within the house's very walls, floors, and ceilings. These unaccountable noises would begin each evening and continue until dawn, denying the family their rest.

The phenomena escalated further. The Mompesson children began to report feeling invisible hands tugging at their bed-clothes or pulling their hair. Even more terrifyingly, the invisible entity seemed to move around objects in the house, including the very drum that had belonged to Drury, creating a sense of unseen chaos.

The Mompessons, in their desperation, sought help from the local clergy, who attempted to dispel the disturbance through prayer and ritual, but to no avail. The relentless drumming and disturbances continued, the unseen entity apparently undeterred by the religious interventions.

As news of the haunting spread beyond Tedworth, the Mompesson house became a site of morbid fascination, drawing scores of curious visitors. Among them was Joseph Glanvill, a chaplain of Charles II and a noted philosopher and author. Intrigued by the Mompesson family's ordeal, Glanvill took upon himself to investigate the haunting.

Glanvill, after witnessing the bizarre events, became convinced that the disturbances were of supernatural origin. He linked the haunting to William Drury, the vagrant drummer, suggesting that Drury was a witch and had cursed the family in retaliation for his lost drum.

Glanvill's endorsement of the Mompesson haunting as a genuine supernatural event lent it significant credibility. His writings on the subject, notably in his book "Saducismus Triumphatus," widely propagated the tale, and it soon became one of the most famous ghost stories in England.

However, not everyone was convinced by Glanvill's interpretation. Sceptics suggested that the haunting was an elaborate hoax, possibly orchestrated by the Mompessons themselves or other interested parties. Others speculated that the phenomena were the result of collective hysteria or the exaggeration of mundane household noises.

The debate over the nature of the Mompesson haunting has endured for centuries, a testament to its enduring fascination. It offers a captivating study of the social and cultural climate of 17th-century England, a time when the line between natural and supernatural, explainable and unexplainable, was often blurred. Whether the disturbances were the result of witchcraft, ghostly activity, deception, or misinterpretation remains a subject of speculation.

What we can conclude is that the Mompesson haunting, like many other tales of witchcraft and the supernatural, served to embody contemporary fears and beliefs. As such, it continues to provide a valuable, if enigmatic, window into a world where the drumbeats of an invisible spectre could resonate with profound implications, echoing through the chambers of a family home and the annals of folklore alike.

Witches of the New Forest: The Burley Coven

As we shift our gaze from the historically harrowing accounts of witch trials and hauntings, we arrive in a quiet, idyllic village nestled within the New Forest, a place where the legacy of witchcraft has taken a decidedly different and contemporary turn. The village of Burley, situated in Hampshire, England, is today synonymous with a unique heritage of witchcraft and wicca practices, making it an essential chapter in our exploration of English witchcraft.

The story of modern witchcraft in Burley begins with an intriguing figure, Sybil Leek, who arrived in the village in the mid-20th century. Leek, with her pet jackdaw perched on her shoulder and her fondness for wearing a long, black cloak, might have seemed a picturesque representation of a stereotypical witch, but her philosophy of witchcraft was anything but.

Born into a family with a longstanding interest in the occult and the metaphysical, Leek was a self-proclaimed witch and astrologer. She was also an ardent advocate for a more enlightened understanding of witchcraft as a nature-based religion rather than an evil force. This philosophy mirrored the broader principles of Wicca, a modern pagan witchcraft religion that had started to emerge around the same time.

Leek's presence in Burley, coupled with her vocal embrace of witchcraft, inevitably drew attention and curiosity. Yet, rather than seeking to inspire fear or awe, Leek used her platform to educate the public about her beliefs. She wrote extensively on astrology, reincarnation, and other esoteric subjects, thereby fostering a more nuanced view of witchcraft.

Following Leek's lead, a group of like-minded individuals formed the first modern coven in Burley. They were drawn together by shared beliefs in nature worship, spirituality, and the pursuit of esoteric knowledge, principles often encapsulated in the Wiccan Rede, 'An it harm none, do what ye will.'

Over time, the Burley coven has grown and evolved. Far removed from the fearful and suspicious portrayals of witches in historical narratives, these modern witches conduct ceremonies known as 'sabbats' throughout the year, focusing particularly on the solstices, equinoxes, and the days halfway between them.

These ceremonies are centred around the celebration of nature and the changing seasons. Rituals often take place outdoors and involve dancing, chanting, and the casting of circles to create sacred space. Members of the coven may also practise spellcasting, although this is far removed from the malevolent curses associated with historical witchcraft. Modern spells are more akin to positive affirmations or prayers, intended to bring healing, protection, or personal growth rather than to harm others.

The Burley coven's practices have not been without

controversy, however. Misunderstandings about Wicca and witchcraft continue to persist, fueled by sensationalised media portrayals and deep-seated cultural and religious prejudices. Members of the coven have sometimes faced discrimination or ridicule for their beliefs and practices.

Yet, the coven has also been instrumental in contributing to a broader cultural shift towards greater acceptance and understanding of alternative religious paths. As part of this trend, Burley has become something of a pilgrimage site for those interested in Wicca and witchcraft, its witch-themed shops and Leek's legacy drawing visitors from around the world.

The Burley coven's commitment to celebrating nature and exploring the mysteries of existence carries forward the rich, often misunderstood, heritage of witchcraft into the present day. Their story illuminates the transformative journey of witchcraft from a source of fear and persecution to a path of spirituality and self-discovery, demonstrating that the narrative of English witchcraft is far from a closed book.

The narrative of the Burley witches, encapsulating both the traditional and contemporary facets of witchcraft, represents a fascinating evolution. It underscores that the tapestry of witchcraft in England is as rich and varied today as it was in centuries past, demonstrating its enduring relevance and appeal. In doing so, it brings our exploration of English witchcraft full circle, from the fear and mystery of the past to a present that seeks understanding and harmony with nature's rhythms.

Afterword

As we draw this exploration of England's witchcraft history to a close, it is evident that the narrative has spanned several centuries, encompassing a diverse range of figures, from the Pendle witches of Lancashire, through Matthew Hopkins, the Witchfinder General, to modern-day witchcraft practitioners in Burley. The thread binding these chapters together reveals a compelling panorama of human nature, cultural beliefs, fear, power, and the constant struggle between acceptance and otherness.

In exploring the infamous Pendle witch trials, we pierced the veil of myth and folklore that has enshrouded the case, seeking to understand the individuals involved as real people, living in extraordinarily challenging times. Figures like Alice Nutter, Elizabeth Southerns, and others emerged from the shadowy realms of legend into the bright light of scrutiny. Their stories remind us that behind every tale of witchcraft lie actual human beings, living in a world driven by complex social, religious, and political dynamics.

Our journey further took us through the Leicester witch trials, involving the cunning women Anne Baker, Joan Willimot, and Ellen Greene. This story provides a unique lens to view the lesser-known aspects of witchcraft and how these women navigated their roles within society. Their tale underscores the variety and flexibility that existed within the framework of 'witchcraft' as understood by people of their time.

The spectre of Matthew Hopkins loomed large as we explored his reign of terror. His actions and methodologies reveal a brutal chapter of England's history, giving us deep insights into the power dynamics, paranoia, and mass hysteria of the time. Yet, as we charted these darker waters, we also encountered figures of hope and resilience, like Jane Wenham and Elizabeth Clarke, who pushed back against the tides of fear and superstition.

King James I's 'Daemonologie' offered us a royal perspective on witchcraft, emphasising how these beliefs and prejudices reached the highest echelons of society. The cases of Eleanor Cobham and Margaret Jourdemayne further underscored this point, demonstrating the dangerous intersection of power, politics, and the supernatural within the royal court.

As we navigated through the ages, we also examined the roles of the cunning folk and pellers. Their stories underline the multifaceted nature of folk magic in England and how its practitioners often walked a fine line between providing a valued service and becoming the subject of suspicion and fear.

Moving beyond the realm of persecution and trial, the Mompesson haunting and the witches of the New Forest shed light on the enduring fascination with the supernatural that persists in England. These accounts, whether we choose to view them as fact or fiction, show us that the allure of the unknown, the uncanny, and the magical is an integral part of the human experience.

The journey you have undertaken in reading "Bewitching Britain: The Hidden Witches of England" is, in essence, a journey through time, a quest for understanding, and an exploration of the diverse facets of human nature. From the fog-shrouded moors of Pendle to the regal splendour of the royal court, from the whispering forests of Burley to the haunted rooms of the Mompesson house, we have traversed an intricate landscape of belief, fear, power, and resistance.

It is my sincere hope that this book has not just informed you about the history of witchcraft in England, but also provoked thought and reflection on the narratives we construct about those who are different, those who challenge societal norms, and those who dare to live according to their own rules. As we close this chapter, remember: history is not just about the past; it is a dialogue with the present, a mirror reflecting our collective fears and hopes, our prejudices and our aspirations.

So, as you leave the world of "Bewitching Britain," carry with you not just the stories and facts contained within these pages, but also the questions they raise and the conversations they inspire. Let them serve as a reminder of our shared humanity, of the power of empathy, and of the infinite capacity of the human spirit to navigate the turbulent currents of history.

About the Author

Lee Brickley is an investigator and author with more than 27 titles currently in publication covering a broad range of subjects including true crime, ancient history, the paranormal, and more.

Born in England, Brickley has been a professional writer for more than two decades. He regularly features in the media due to wide interest in his work, and he has made numerous TV appearances.

For more books from this author, simply search

"Lee Brickley" on Amazon.